Prima Ballerina

Also edited by Miriam Hodgson

The Teens Book of Love Stories

Take Your Knee Off My Heart

Heartache

Mother's Day

Prima Ballerina

A book of ballet stories

Edited by Miriam Hodgson
Illustrated by Kate Aldous

Methuen Children's Books

First published in Great Britain 1992
by Methuen Children's Books
an imprint of Reed Consumer Books Limited
Michelin House, 81 Fulham Road, London SW3 6RB
and Auckland, Melbourne, Singapore and Toronto

Reprinted 1993

Stand Tall copyright © 1992 Marjorie Darke
The Third Dancer copyright © 1992 Jean Richardson
And Olly Did Too copyright © 1992 Jamila Gavin
Falling Star copyright © 1992 Vivien Alcock
Little Swan copyright © 1992 Adèle Geras
I Don't Want to Dance! copyright © 1992 Bel Mooney
The First Night Surprise copyright © 1992 Susan Hampshire
(This story is based on material in *Lucy Jane at the Ballet*
by Susan Hampshire, first published by William Collins)
Poppy Smith — Prima Ballerina copyright © 1992 Jean Ure
Illustrations copyright © 1992 Kate Aldous

The rights of the authors listed here to be identified as the
authors of these stories have been asserted by them in
accordance with the Copyright, Designs and Patent Act, 1988

This volume copyright © 1992 Reed International Books Limited

ISBN 0 416 18701 3

A CIP catalogue record for this book is available at the British Library

Printed in Great Britain by Butler and Tanner Ltd., Frome and London

Contents

Stand Tall

Marjorie Darke

Kaye hung over the end of her bed slowly gathering up the middle of the valance frill, and fixed it with a safety pin. Upside down, she stared into the special secret darkness under her bed.

There it was. The Stage – curtains raised for the performance to begin!

Little fizzes of excitement shot down her neck.

'Dum diddle diddle, dee pom . . .' Kaye hummed to help the orchestra as she lowered

Amelita Boxworthia into the wings of the under-bed-stage.

Amelita was glued to one of Gran's old knitting needles to make it easier to push her about. Kaye didn't know where the name came from. It had fallen, ready-made, into her head just as she finished sticking the dancer on to the needle . . .

AMELITA BOXWORTHIA!

Bright shining poster letters. Like those she had seen outside the birthday-treat theatre. Not *her* birthday – Lynne next door's. Lynne had been going to Muz Cara's ballet classes for three months now. The treat had been a theatre visit to see the Royal Ballet Company dance something called *Swan Lake*. Lynne had asked Kaye to go as well.

'Oo . . . please,' Kaye said.

From the moment they entered the theatre she loved everything. Enormous curtains sweeping back. Orchestra striking up. Huge shadowy stage. Mysterious forest scenery. Best of all was Odile. She seemed to be the Swan Princess's double but had a better costume, Kaye thought. Black net covered with spangles. Black feathers on her head.

Of course Amelita didn't belong to the Royal Ballet Company. She wasn't born until a week later when Kaye cut her out of the *Radio Times*. Which was when the name dropped into her head.

And that was that.

Not long afterwards Grant Lightfoot turned up on some fancy wrapping paper to be Amelita's partner.

Then Ivy Wart skidded in. From the moment Kaye cut her from the back of the cornflakes box, Ivy did as she pleased. Sliding here and there. Insisting on all the baddie parts – grumpy ghosts, slimy stepmothers, even a wicked sausage. The sausage was Ivy's favourite because it was greasy which meant she could slither about instead of learning the steps that Kaye-the-dance-teacher had worked out for her.

Over the summer holidays the company grew. Six chorus girls – Becky, Lou, Olive, Jude, May and Paulettina – on their points side by side, glued to another knitting needle. Two clowns with no names off an old Christmas card. Fred Strongarm, acrobat, (free gift with bubble gum). The four cowboys on horseback Kaye pinched from her brother when he wasn't looking. Several old-fashioned cardboard animal dancers were another free gift – from Gran's allsorts drawer. Last to join the company was Princess Sweetbriar. She arrived in some junk-mail post.

Then the serious trouble began.

From the word go Amelita and the Princess quarrelled because they both wanted to dance the star parts. No matter how Kaye scolded they took no notice. She tried standing them in corners, banishing them to their shoebox, even tying them back to back, so they couldn't glare at each other.

Nothing worked.

Hanging over the bed now, Kaye could hear Princess Sweetbriar's squeaky grumble and almost poked herself in the eye with Amelita's needle trying to stop up her ears.

'Why don't you shut up?' She gave Amelita a shake.

Out of spite Amelita fell backwards making creases in her legs.

Kaye scowled.

Ever since the summer holidays ended and term began, the whole company seemed out of sorts. The chorus wanted to dance separately. The clowns wouldn't tumble. The animal dancers tumbled in all the wrong places and knocked Fred Strongarm into the audience.

Worst of all were Amelita's tantrums when Things went Wrong. Things often did go Wrong because Kaye didn't have enough hands to raise the curtain, guide several needles and shine the spotlight torch, all at the same time.

'Behave yourself!' Smoothing Amelita's bent legs, she lay flat and tried to juggle her across the stage.

The orchestra struck up. 'Dum diddle diddle, pom pom lah . . . OH STINK!' Flicking on the spotlight Kaye dropped the torch which rolled to the very back of the bed.

'SHUT UP, YOU KNOCK-KNEED GIT!' she yelled at Amelita, who had gone into one of her worst tantrums. But Amelita wouldn't listen.

Kaye flung her across the room, dived for the torch, hooked her T-shirt on a bedspring, hit her head on the bed end and finally kicked the shoebox spilling dancers every which way.

Tears rising, she stared at the disaster. Then scrambling up, she ran downstairs, outside and in next door without stopping.

Lynne, wearing a leotard and dancing slippers, was standing in front of the long mirror in the hall. She took no notice as the door burst open; she was clutching the radiator and trying to do something impossible with her feet.

'Willyoucomeandhelpworkthedancers,' Kaye gabbled before her nerve crumbled. She had never mentioned her secret theatre to anyone before. The sudden feeling something was spoiled made her gulp and sniff. But if the theatre was to work properly there *must* be another backstage hand.

'Look!' Lynne puffed proudly, getting her heels together at last, toes sticking out in the opposite direction.

Kaye glared. 'What's that supposed to be?'

Lynne said something that sounded like, 'Sinky Em position,' and fell over.

'Stinky Em?' Kaye said rudely, scrubbing under her nose with her sleeve.

'*Cinquième*, I said.' Lynne got up, rather red. 'It's French meaning fifth position.'

'Pooh . . . anybody can do that!' Kaye said, not believing herself. She spun round and round

11

several times to show there were things she could do.

'Bet you can't do the splits.' Lynne began sliding her legs wider and wider apart until she was sitting on the floor, puffing and blowing as if she had run ten miles.

Secretly Kaye thought Lynne was probably right, but felt obliged to try. Halfway down she heard an ominous ripping noise as her jeans split. 'If I had a leotard I could,' she said, not believing that either.

'Ask your mum to buy you one, why don't you?' Lynne was suddenly enthusiastic. 'I know . . . why don't you get her to ask Muz Cara if you can join the ballet class. Your mum's giving me a lift this evening. You can come too. You might be able to start straight away. It'd be fun to go to classes together.'

This was the first Kaye had heard about any lift, and remembering Muz Cara's big calf muscles and trumpet voice telling everyone to:

'Stand Tall!'

wasn't so sure about the fun.

'What, me?' her voice squeaked.

'Who else?' Lynne turned back to the mirror, arms raised. 'That's *cinquième* as well.'

Kaye opened her mouth to say, 'Stinky Em,' again but instead copied Lynne, arms circling her head.

'Very good!' Lynne sounded as if she really meant it.

Kaye blushed. Keeping arms and hands where they were, she tried to get her feet into the *cinquième* position but knew she couldn't. A picture of Odile, spotlight shimmering on her black spangles, opened in her head. Odile pointed one toe and swept her arms down and back in a deep graceful curtsey.

Almost without knowing, Kaye imitated. It was like watching a film, the movements unrolling, and she *was* Odile in the sharp spotlight. The rest of the stage lay in shadow. Below in the orchestra pit, the violins shivered out a chain of silvery notes. Somewhere beyond, the unseen audience sat watching the new young star dancer. Alone under the glittering spotlight, her arms swept down and back with perfect . . .

'Cor!' Lynne said. 'Where did you learn that?'

Kaye gulped again – jolted back into Lynne's hall with the mirror and radiator and the split in her jeans letting in a draught.

She had really been on stage . . . inside Odile's skin!

Cold goosebumps prickled her arms. But the admiration in Lynne's eyes was warming. Before she could think of the right words to explain what had happened, a shout came from the kitchen:

'Tea's ready, Lynne. Hurry up or you'll be late for class!'

Lynne began pushing Kaye towards the door. 'I'll have to go. Don't forget what I said.' And just as she was about to shut her out: 'What was it you came round to ask me?'

'Oh . . . nothing. It doesn't matter.' Kaye realised that the under-bed-stage was still her secret. Somehow it didn't seem important now. A brand new idea gripped her.

Why not be the dancer instead of just the backstage hand!

Kaye pelted for home, crashed in through the back door shouting:

'MumLynnesayscanIgotoballetwithherohpleasecanI?'

Autumn term rushed into winter. Muz Cara's Show was booked in the church hall for the two days before Christmas. This very evening was First Night. Lynne, in wonderful rainbow tights and feather cap, was being fastened into the rest of her bluebird costume. Various bright flowers stood in a line waiting for Muz Cara to shuffle them into place in the stage garden. A caterpillar and a butterfly giggled behind a flat tree trunk, close to a small, shivering, silent moth.

'QUIET!' Muz Cara trumpeted.

Making more noise than anyone, the moth thought, staring bleakly sideways on to the stage.

The church hall was new and had a proper stage with scenery and curtains like a real theatre. There was a smell of face paint and dust. Out in the front the audience was chatting and laughing.

But none of this mattered. What did matter was that the moth couldn't remember a single step of

her dance. The more she tried, the further away danced the dance. Her insides quaked. She felt sick. Had Amelita Boxworthia felt this scared on her First Night?

Warm hands rested on her shoulder.

The moth looked up. 'I can't remember . . .' she began, and saw Muz Cara's emerald eyes twinkle down, her mouth smile up.

'Stand Tall, Kaye. All right?' Muz Cara gave her a little push.

And it *was* all right. Kaye ran on stage as the

16

piano called, scattering musical instructions like a pattern over the floor, telling her feet what to do. The fright fell away.

She was dancing!

The Third Dancer

Jean Richardson

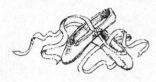

The first time Tamara was taken to the ballet was the last time her father danced in a performance.

His farewell was a very grand occasion. As the guests of honour, Tamara, her mother and her brother Lev sat on little gilt chairs in the splendid privacy of a box of their own.

High above them, in the domed heavens of the opera house, sparkled the lights of a great crystal chandelier. Around and below them were tiers of red plush seats, soon to be filled with an audience who had come especially to say goodbye to one of their favourite dancers.

It was a magical new world to Tamara. Everyone looked so unlike their everyday selves that she and Lev, afraid that they might miss him, kept asking, 'Where's Papa? Which one's Papa?'

Papa didn't come on until the second act, and even then Tamara kept losing sight of him as he wove in and out of the other dancers.

But there was no mistaking his solo. He flew through the air, twirling round twice before landing as surely as a bird on one foot and then whirling round and round so fast that he dissolved into thin air like Lev's spinning top. There was a

deafening burst of applause, and Tamara and Lev
stamped their feet like the people in the gallery
and hammered excitedly on the rail of the box.

And of course there were encores and presents
and speeches, and Papa had to bow to the
Emperor in the Imperial box before thanking the
rest of the audience.

After such a night, which they talked about for
days, there was only one thing Tamara wanted to

be: a dancer. But to her amazement, her father was against the idea.

'But why, Papa,' she asked in dismay, 'why can't I have lessons?'

He was sterner and more distant than she had ever seen him. 'I think you're too young,' he said, and left the room before she could say any more.

But Tamara was sure that seven wasn't too young for lessons, and she wanted to dance now. There must be some other reason, though she couldn't imagine what, why such a marvellous dancer as her father, who was now going to teach other people to dance, didn't want his daughter to follow in his footsteps. Even tears, which in the past she'd found quite good for persuading him, were useless. In fact, they made him so angry that she was quite scared of him.

Her mother, however, thought Tamara would make a beautiful dancer, though she knew it was no good arguing about it.

'You won't get round your father that way,' she said. 'He's a very obstinate man, and he doesn't change his mind easily. But I've an idea . . .'

The 'idea' turned out to be private lessons from Aunt Vera, a friend of Tamara's mother who had once been a ballerina.

'You'll get individual tuition from a great dancer,' her mother said, 'and if Aunt Vera thinks you show promise, I'm sure Papa will be impressed.'

To be honest, Tamara was a little disappointed with Aunt Vera's lessons. She'd pictured herself bounding through the air and whirling round and round like her father had done.

Instead, Aunt Vera made her hold on to a bar fixed to the back of the dining-room door and do very dull exercises with her feet and arms. When she complained, Aunt Vera explained that this was the way even the most famous dancers trained, and that they went on doing these same exercises all their dancing lives to keep their limbs supple.

Tamara sighed, and persevered. If this was what she had to do to become a dancer, she would do it.

But sometimes at home, when she was supposed to be having a rest in her room and she heard her mother playing the piano, Tamara would put on her dancing shoes and pretend she was a ballerina. Her mother had taken her to see *Swan Lake* and *Les Sylphides*, and she knew now that swans and sylphs danced on their toes, or *pointes*, as they were called, spun across the stage in pirouettes while balancing on one leg and floated through the air as effortlessly as though they had wings. It was so much more romantic and thrilling than Aunt Vera's boring positions.

One day her mother was practising a Chopin nocturne. As Tamara listened to the dreamy music, her bedroom seemed bathed in moonlight and she moved like the fragile heroines of her

21

dreams. She was so wrapped up in the music that she didn't notice the door open, and it was only when the music ended that she was aware of a figure watching her in the shadows.

It was her father.

'Oh, Papa, I . . .' For a moment, Tamara was lost for words, and then excuses came tumbling out. 'I didn't mean to be naughty. It's just that . . . that I want to dance so much.'

Her father sat down on her bed. He didn't look angry, but rather sad, as though in some way she had wounded him.

'It's all right,' he said. 'I understand – though I'm not sure if you're old enough to understand me.'

'I'll try. I'm quite good at reading and I can add up and take away. And Aunt Vera thinks I could be a dancer . . .' Too late Tamara remembered that the lessons with Aunt Vera were meant to be a secret.

'So, Vera's in the plot too, is she? I suppose that was your mother's doing. She's never been a dancer, so she doesn't know how much it hurts.'

'You mean it makes your feet hurt. Aunt Vera told me I won't be able to dance on my *pointes* for ages, and even then, I'll have to be very careful.'

'She's right, you will, but I wasn't thinking about feet and muscles and all the physical things that can hurt. No, what I wanted to spare you, what I hoped I could spare you, was all the heartache that goes with being a dancer. You think it's so beautiful and glamorous, like it is on the stage, but behind the scenes it's very different. Dancers have to practise every day, even if they don't feel like dancing. There are so many intrigues and disappointments, and even if you're any good, like I was, it's for so short a time. I may seem grown-up to you, but I'm still a young man, yet I'm too old to be a prince any more. I enjoy teaching, but every time I go to rehearsals, I long to change places with my students.'

Tamara put her arms round her father. It hadn't occurred to her that he'd been made to give up dancing. How much it must hurt to have to watch other people doing the one thing that mattered most of all to you.

'Won't they let you dance any more?'

'No. My contract was for twenty years, and after twenty years' service, most dancers retire. One or two are sometimes kept on, but I wasn't one of the lucky ones. You need friends in the right places, and ballet-master Petipa doesn't like me. Your mother says it's my own fault, because I used to make fun of his acting. Lesson one, don't upset the people who matter.'

'But you're not sorry you were a dancer, are you?'

'Are you trying to catch me out, my little Tata! My father was a dancer, and I saw what happened to him, but it didn't make any difference, just as it won't make any difference to you. It's in the blood, and you'll be the third generation of this

family to go on the stage.'

'You mean I can go on having lessons! You don't mind any more!' Tamara flung her arms round her father's neck and kissed him.

'I suppose so. But if you're really serious about dancing, you must do it properly.'

'I will, I will. I promise. I'll do everything Aunt Vera says.'

'Vera,' said her father, 'was an excellent dancer, but only the best is good enough for my daughter. I shall teach you myself. And I warn you, I'm very strict. It'll be a test of how much you really want to dance.'

'Oh, Papa!'

After her father had gone downstairs to tell her mother, Tamara sat on her bed, feeling trembly and a little frightened. It had started as a lovely game. Now she saw that being the third dancer in the family was going to be very hard work.

This story was suggested by incidents in *Theatre Street*, the delightful autobiography of the great Russian dancer, Tamara Karsavina.

And Olly Did Too

Jamila Gavin

Jenny said, 'When I grow up, I'm going to be a ballet dancer.'

Her younger brother Olly said, 'I will too,' but everyone laughed and took no notice.

Jenny tried to look like a ballet dancer. She always wore her hair swept tightly back into a bun; she always stood with a very straight back; she always held her head up high to show off her long neck; and when she walked, she turned her feet out, just like ballet dancers do.

Olly rushed about like a wild thing, wearing his track suit and trainers. He kept jumping and leaping and kicking his legs in the air, like a frisky horse.

'Are you trying to be a footballer, Olly?' people asked.

'No,' said Olly, 'I'm going to be a ballet dancer!' Everyone roared with laughter, because Olly was such a little toughie with his spiky hair and rough and tumbling body.

Every Wednesday after school, Mum took Jenny to her ballet lesson. Olly went too, but only to watch because Mum couldn't leave him at

27

home on his own.

Olly used to fidget. He watched Jenny in her black leotard and pink, fluffy, cross-over cardigan. He kicked his feet against the chair while she put on her shining pink ballet shoes and crisscrossed the pink satin ribbons round her ankles.

Mum had to rap Olly across the knees and tell him to keep still. In the end, she would send him right away to the back of the hall with a box of action toys, to keep him out of mischief. But as soon as the piano started thumping out the tunes for the dancers to do their exercises, Olly did them too where no one could see him.

Every day, Jenny practised her ballet movements in the kitchen. She would hold the back of a chair and then call out the French words for each position:

'*Première position* ... *plié* ... *jeté* ... *attitude* ...'

Olly did too. He pointed his toes and bent his knees and lifted his leg forwards and backwards; he raised his arm and curved his hands and always remembered to look in whatever direction his fingers went. But nobody noticed. They thought he was fooling about.

Having a ballet dancer in the family was such hard work. There always seemed to be a show to rehearse or an exam to prepare. Father couldn't count the number of times he had driven Jenny to

and from draughty church halls; and Mother couldn't remember how many costumes she'd made. Olly had never known a time when the house wasn't scattered with bits of stiff net for tutus, satin and silks for bodices and ribbons, or when every surface wasn't covered with boxes of pins and buttons and sequins.

Olly liked dressing up too, but everyone thought he was just messing around. He would grab the old green velvet curtains Mum had kept by for cutting up, and swing them round his shoulders like a cloak; and how everybody

29

laughed when he put on his mother's black leather boots which almost went up to his thighs.

'What on earth do you think you look like in those!' exclaimed Jenny, scornfully.

'That's what princes wear, isn't it?' retorted Olly.

When it was Jenny's birthday, they took her to the ballet. Olly went too, because Granny couldn't babysit that night. Everyone thought Olly would hate going to the theatre and they hoped he wouldn't wriggle and keep asking to go to the toilet. Mum said he would probably be bored and fall asleep.

When they arrived at the theatre, there were lots and lots of girls wearing velvet dresses with broad sashes. All had their hair swept under Alice-bands or twisted into net buns; and all were standing like swans, holding their heads up very high and with their feet turned out. There were many boys too, trying to look grand and grown-up, but Olly didn't notice. He couldn't stand still long enough to notice. He was so excited. He couldn't wait to get inside and see the dancers.

'One day,' whispered Mum proudly to Jenny, 'everyone will be queueing to see you!'

Olly said, 'Will they come and see me too?' But everyone laughed.

They went in through the glass doors into the foyer with the red velvet plush carpet. Those who hadn't already bought tickets were queueing hopefully, while others, like Dad, fumbled in jackets and pockets for theirs.

'You're in the upper circle,' said a man in black and white evening dress examining their tickets. 'You take the left staircase.'

Jenny walked sedately up the stairs, sliding her hand along the gold banister like a princess. She didn't look to the right or the left, but straight ahead, as though a handsome prince was waiting for her at the top.

Olly hopped and jumped and would have raced up two at a time if his legs had been long enough. He couldn't wait to get inside.

'Hurry up, Jenny! Hurry up!' he begged.

'Behave yourself, Olly. We're going to the ballet, not a football match,' said Mum sternly.

At last they were inside. At last they found their seats. They were rather high up, but had a perfect view right down to the stage. Dad turned, to warn Olly to sit still and not to dare make a noise, but he didn't need to. Olly was leaning forward watching the musicians coming into the dark orchestral pit below the stage. First the harpist came in, because he took the longest to tune all those strings; then came a horn player, because she wanted to practise a difficult bit; and one by one, the violinist and cellists, the clarinetists and flautists and all the other players came in with their instruments.

The leader of the orchestra entered with his violin under his arm. The audience clapped and when he had bowed and sat down, the oboist played an A and all the players tuned into it.

Finally, the conductor made his entrance. He climbed up on to a rostrum and bowed to the audience while everybody clapped. Then the conductor faced his players.

The lights went down. There was a huge hush, and with a wave of a baton the music started. The great, heavy curtain rose slowly upwards.

Olly never moved a muscle; he might have been a statue, his body was so still, and his eyes so fixed. But his soul heaved like an ocean. His spirit flew like a bird. It soared across the darkened auditorium; it wafted among the white, billowing skirts of the girls, and sprang up, up, up with the shining princes in their glittering jackets. The dancers no longer seemed to be ordinary human beings, but enchanted people; magic people; the way their bodies created changing shapes and patterns, sometimes moving like one body; arms lifting and falling, legs bending and stretching, backs arching and heads turning, all at the same time. And the way the stage was no longer just a wooden stage, but in one scene it was brilliantly lit as a magnificent royal palace, and in the next, it was a dark, menacing forest. If it was real, then Olly wanted to be up there with them, dancing and leaping to the lilting rhythms of the music; but if it was a dream, and it seemed to be a dream, then he never never never wanted to wake up.

After that, Olly was always dreaming: day
dreams and night dreams. Sometimes he dreamed
in school, when he should have been doing his
sums, but instead, he found himself floating up to
the ceiling. Suddenly he was astride a black horse
and galloping across a night sky; a bejewelled
turban of silk was wound round his head, and a
cloak of darkness whirled behind him. Then he
was a hunter, stalking through a forest hung with
diamonds and pearls, where long-legged spiders
spun webs of silver, and strange-winged gnomes
sprang through the air. Sometimes he was a
magician or a king, or simply just a dancer
spinning through space.

Most of all, he dreamt he was up on that stage,

where the lights glittered above him like stars; where he could hear the squeak of the ballet shoes as the dancers pirouetted and twirled, the swish of costumes and the clouds of music which rose from the pit below, flowing into his arms and legs.

One day, Mum and Dad took Jenny to an audition. It was to choose the best dancers to go to a special ballet school. Jenny didn't really want to go because it meant she would have to miss her riding lesson. All of a sudden, Jenny had become mad about horses, and wasn't so sure now that she wanted to be a dancer.

'Of course you must go, Jenny,' said Mother with a frown. 'You've always wanted to be a ballet dancer, and this may be your one big chance.'

Olly went too, because he couldn't be left on his own.

An ancient lady, who looked about a hundred years old, leant her chin on a silver-tipped cane and watched every child with the eye of a hawk. Olly had been told to sit quietly at the back, but though he was quiet, he couldn't sit still. When the children were told to stand, he stood; when they were told to walk, he walked; he walked just as the princes had walked that day at the ballet, with heads held proudly and one arm lifted out before him, making a noble gesture.

He walked down the side aisle, until he was

nearly at the front. Nobody had noticed, because all eyes were fixed on the children who were auditioning – except the old lady. Somehow, she noticed. Perhaps she had eyes at the back of her head. Perhaps she was a witch, and her back tingled when somebody danced. She seemed to see everything, though no one knew. Suddenly she got up – or did she spring? For as she got to her feet, she was no longer just an old lady, she was a dancer. Olly stopped, and shrank, watching, into the shadows.

She walked along the line of children, pointing with her silver cane. She studied their fronts and their backs; their thighs and their legs; their knees and their ankles, and she even made them walk barefoot, so that she could examine their toes.

'You may have to look as delicate as flowers, but you have to be as strong as tigers,' she muttered.

'I'm strong!' exclaimed Olly, suddenly stepping out boldly before her.

'Olly!' hissed his mother, very shocked. 'Don't be rude. Go and play with your cars at the back of the hall.'

But the old, old lady waved her silver cane at him.

'Yes, I've been watching you. Let me have a look at you, my boy. Strip off down to your underpants.'

Some children giggled, but Olly did as he was asked.

'Walk across the stage!' she ordered. Olly walked.

'Point your toes, bend your knees, stand on one leg, jump in the air.' Olly did all those things.

About fifty children had come to the audition that day, but they knew that only six could be chosen. At the end of every session, a person with a large notebook would say to the parents of each child, 'We'll let you know.'

So they had to go home and wait. They waited and waited. Mum was longing to know whether Jenny had been chosen, and watched for the post every day. But Jenny hardly noticed the time going by. She was clamouring for a pair of riding boots and jodhpurs and she was asking if she could go to pony camp in the summer.

At last, one day, a letter came through the door. It was from the ballet school. Mother opened it with trembling fingers.

'Well,' exclaimed Dad with breathless impatience, 'has Jenny got in?'

Mum didn't answer. She read the letter once, then she read it again.

'For goodness sake, tell me!' begged Dad. 'What do they say?'

Finally, Mum replied in a small voice, 'They say they want Olly!'

'Oh, good!' yelled Olly, leaping into the air. 'I always wanted to be a dancer!'

'Does that mean I don't have to go to ballet classes any more?' cried Jenny with a grin. 'Oh good! I'd much rather go horse-riding instead!'

Olly shut his eyes tight. He imagined himself up on the stage. He could feel the warmth of the lights and the smell of the face paints; he could hear the music casting its spell over him, so that his feet began to twitch. Before him was a wide, empty space. With a whoop of joy, he gave a giant leap. With his arms and legs outstretched, he was like a tiger in full flight.

That year, a specially chosen group of children went to the ballet school to train as dancers. Olly went too.

Falling Star
Vivien Alcock

I was so happy. I wanted to dance in the wet streets, singing, 'They've chosen me! They've chosen me!'

But my brother would have said I was showing off. Ted is always cross when Mum gets him to fetch me home from my ballet class on Tuesdays. It's not my fault she won't let me walk home alone, not in winter when it's dark early. I can't help being only nine.

Ted hates ballet, anyway. When Mum took us to see *Swan Lake* three years ago, he grumbled and fidgeted, picked his nose and kicked the seat in front of him, until the lady turned round and complained. Mum said she was ashamed of him. I hadn't even noticed.

My eyes were dazzled. I saw nothing but the dancers leaping and spinning, caught like butterflies in a golden net of light.

When it was over, I didn't clap. I just sat there, staring.

'What's the matter, Liz?' Mum asked. 'You look terribly pale. I hope you're not sickening for something.'

'I'm going to be a ballerina when I grow up,' I said.

My mind was quite made up. All I wanted to do was dance. Now and for ever.

It was a pity I didn't seem to be very good at it. Mum enrolled me at the Pelling School of Dance and Drama, Tuesdays and Thursdays after school. Everyone there was better than me, except poor Pam Greene, who's hopeless. Her legs are too short and fat; mine are too long and thin. They got tangled up in the little running steps. I kept stumbling. Once I fell right over, crash bang on the floor. Everyone laughed.

'You're not hurt, are you, dear?' Miss Isobel Pelling said, helping me up. 'Try not to get so excited. Don't throw your legs about so wildly. This isn't a football match.'

I hated her.

Then she said something I couldn't hear to Mrs Woods, who plays the piano. Mrs Woods sighed and shook her head. I hated her too. I just knew they were saying I would never be any good, and should they tell my mother not to waste her money. I wanted to cry.

But that was last term. Tonight I loved them both. I loved the whole world. I even loved Ted . . . I looked at him sideways. Should I tell him? He wouldn't be interested . . . But I was so excited, I had to tell someone.

'They've chosen me! *Me!*' I said, doing a little *pas seul* round a puddle. 'I'm to be in the

Christmas ballet!'

'You were in it last year,' he complained. 'I was there, remember? Mum made me come. You were a snowball –'

'A snow fairy,' I said coldly.

He's a beast, I thought. Always making fun of me, just because I'm younger. Why should I care what he thinks, the brainless slob? Except that he's the only brother I've got, and I can't help

41

wishing that once, just once, he'd be proud of me.

'That wasn't the proper Christmas ballet,' I told him. 'That's just something the school puts on each year for the mums and dads to watch. Only the babies and the juniors who haven't been chosen for the ballet take part. This is quite different. It's the senior show. They only take six of us from the juniors. Miss Pelling says it's a great honour to be chosen.'

I didn't tell him there were only seven in the junior class this year, and I was the last they'd picked. Even then, they'd hesitated between me and Pam Greene, who dances like an elephant with five left feet. She didn't cry when she was left out. She gave me a wobbly smile and said, 'Well done, Liz.' It made me feel *awful*, because I couldn't help feeling happy, too. I thought she was very brave. But that's show business, I suppose. You have to take the rough with the smooth.

'It's going to be in the town hall,' I told Ted. 'On the proper stage where they have the pantomimes. And somebody's coming from the *Hornsey Journal* to take photographs.'

'Big deal,' he said, yawning. 'And what are you going to be this time?'

'A star,' I mumbled.

'What?' He stared at me in surprise. He was impressed at last. 'Really, Liz? Well done! You must be good. Who'd have thought it! My sister only nine years old and already a star.'

It wasn't a lie. I *was* going to be a star. All six of us juniors were going to be stars, only not the sort he imagined. We were to be twinkle, twinkle little stars in silver tutus, dancing around a ballerina moon against a dark-blue canvas sky. Right at the back of the stage, that's where we were going to be, on a raised platform painted to look like rooftops.

In front of us, seven seniors in furry leotards, with painted whiskery faces and big pointed ears fixed to their heads, were to dance to a tune from *Cats*, while half-hidden in the background, we skipped round the ballerina moon.

'Skip, I said, not trip, Liz,' Miss Pelling told me, as we rehearsed. 'Do try and concentrate on what you're doing. Keep within those chalk marks, that's the size the platform will be. We can't have you falling down among the cats.'

She made me nervous. I had enough to worry about already. Ted still thought I was going to be one of the ballerinas, as if I could be at my age. I'm not even allowed to dance on my *pointes* yet, in case I damage my toes while my bones are still bendy. Ted doesn't know anything about ballet.

Mum does. She made my costume, all silver net and sequins, with a painted headdress with five shining points. I asked her not to tell Ted I was only going to be a cardboard and tinsel star, one of six, because I knew he'd laugh himself sick.

'But, darling, he'll find out. He's coming with us —'

43

'Tell him he can't!'

'Liz, how can I? He offered to come off his own bat. I didn't even have to hint. Besides, it's a great thing to have been chosen to be in the senior ballet.'

'Ted won't think so. He'll think it's funny. He'll call me Twinkle-Toes or something sick-making for the rest of my life. I wish they'd chosen Pam Greene and not me! I really do!'

Yet sometimes it was fun. At the dress rehearsal, with everyone in costume: the cats, us stars and the shining ballerina moon, with the spotlights falling down on us like golden streamers – then all the magic came back. It was fairyland again and I was part of it.

'Isn't it wonderful!' I said to Miss Pelling, when we were all changing to go home.

She smiled rather anxiously. 'Don't get over-excited tomorrow, Liz,' she said. 'We don't want you falling over, do we?'

She shouldn't have said that. I kept thinking of it when we waited in the wings the next night, exchanging nervous smiles. Stomachs somersaulting . . . legs turning to limp string . . . wanting to be sick . . .

The music began. The curtain rose. There we were dancing round the pirouetting moon, while the cats leaped and whirled below us.

I swear it wasn't my fault. Somebody's foot caught my ankle, and I went flying. I missed the ballerina moon by a millimetre, shot off the edge of our platform and landed on the stage below. My feet skidded wildly on the boards.

I mustn't fall down! *I mustn't!* Miss Pelling would never forgive me. Ted would never stop laughing at me. Mum would be ashamed.

I waved my arms like a windmill, trying to keep my balance. Round and round I tottered, swerving to avoid crashing into the leaping cats. I was getting giddy. I grabbed at a rope: it turned out to be a tabby tail. It came off in my hand. The cat it belonged to, now a manx, hissed at me and pushed me towards the wings. I hit the curtains and subsided gently on to the floor. The dusty velvet billowed out and hid me from the roaring audience.

Somebody pulled me farther back into the wings. It was Miss Pelling. 'Never mind, Liz,' she sighed. 'You're not hurt, are you?'

'No.'

But I was hurt. I was shamed, my future career was in ruins. Never would I dance again, never! I wished I were dead.

Mr Dawson from Drama tiptoed over and crouched down beside me.

'Brilliant,' he whispered, patting my shoulder and beaming at me. 'Absolutely brilliant. Why aren't you in my drama class? You're a born clown.'

I didn't want to be in a circus, having buckets of water thrown at me. I wanted to be on a stage, having bouquets of flowers. Yet he seemed so

pleased with me, as if I'd done something clever.

The audience was pleased with me too. When the show was over, and the dancers took their bows, they shouted for me. 'Where's the falling star?' Somebody pushed me forward and everyone cheered. I could see Ted clapping like mad and Mum smiling. I couldn't understand it.

'They thought it was intentional,' Miss Pelling explained to me later. 'They thought you were *meant* to be a shooting star. I wonder if we should keep it in . . . No, no, too risky, I'm afraid. Pity. It really was very funny.'

'I could easily do it again,' I offered. 'I'm going to be a comedienne when I grow up. I thought I'd change over to Drama next term. And I might take singing lessons so I can be in musical comedy.'

'That's a splendid idea, Liz,' she said, thankfully.

Little Swan

Adèle Geras

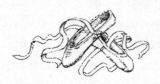

'Louisa,' said my little sister at breakfast one day, 'I want both of you to call me Louisa, now that I'm going to be a little swan in the dancing display.'

'Cygnet,' I said. 'That's the proper name for a little swan.'

If I had been a piece of bread, the look Weezer gave me would have turned me into toast on the spot.

'I know,' she said, 'but you don't call them cygnets in ballet. You call them little swans. Miss Matting said so. It's like *Swan Lake*. There's a "Dance of the Little Swans" in that.'

'But your dance isn't *Swan Lake*,' I said. 'It's just Miss Matting's silly little dancing display. Surely you could be called Weezer for that?'

I could see the anger boiling up inside her. I expect she was wondering if she could stab me with the butter knife. Mum saw it too, though, and stepped in to calm things down.

'Stop it at once, you two. Annie, you're just peeved because you've never been in a dancing display. If Louisa wants to be called that, then that's what we'll call her. Miss Matting's displays

are always of a very high standard, in any case.
They're not silly and little at all.'

'Sorry,' I said, knowing that Weezer would
sulk all day if I didn't apologize. She's one of
those people who can easily stay in a rotten mood
for days and days, and I needed her this afternoon
to be the princess in a game my friend Josie and I
were going to play, called Royal People.

'That's all right,' she said. 'I expect you're
jealous because you're too tall ever to be a real
ballet dancer.'

I didn't bother to point out that jumping
around in a sticky-out white skirt and pink satin
shoes wasn't my idea of fun. Instead I said:

'When is the display? Can Josie come on our
spare ticket?'

'It's on Saturday, and there isn't a spare ticket
any more,' said Weezer. 'I'm going to give it to
someone.' She tried to look mysterious. I thought
for a bit about the person she might have chosen.
We always had an extra ticket for things, because
our mum and dad were divorced, and Dad had
moved to another town. This happened three
years ago, and Weezer and I were very sad about
it at first, but we'd got used to it now. It was only
when things like dancing displays came up that
we sometimes became gloomy again.

'Can't you guess?' she asked. 'Go on. Try.'

I said: 'Nicola.'

'No.'

'Mrs Walsh?' (Mrs Walsh was Weezer's teacher

in Top Infants.)

'No.'

'I give up.'

Weezer beamed. 'Mrs Posnansky!' she announced.

'But you don't know her,' I said. Mrs Posnansky lived across the road and a few doors down from our house.

'I know who she is. I've seen her and smiled and said hello sometimes.'

'But why her?'

'She's Russian. Russians love the ballet. Miss Matting says so.'

'That's not a very good reason. There must be something else.'

'Well, she looks like a grandmother, and we haven't got one, and besides, Ben told me she keeps a box of chocolates in her sideboard and every time they go there, she takes it out and gives them some.'

I laughed. Ben was Josie's younger brother. We used to be able to persuade him to join in games of Royal People as the prince, but he won't play it any more.

My mother said: 'You girls should be getting off to school now. You can talk about Mrs Posnansky on the way. I think it's a very good idea to invite her. I'm sure she'd love to come. You can go over after school and ask her, Weezer dear.'

'Louisa,' said Weezer, glowering.

'Sorry, sorry,' said Mum. 'Of course. Louisa it is.'

On the way to school, I said: 'What time are you going to see Mrs Posnansky?'

'I thought we'd go at about 4.30,' said Weezer.

'We?'

She stopped in the middle of the pavement.

'You've got to come with me, Annie. I'm too young to go on my own.'

Weezer was seven and a half, and Mum and I sometimes said she'd be running the world by the time she was ten. Certainly, we mostly ended up doing what she wanted for the sake of peace.

'OK,' I said. 'I'll come, but you're doing all the talking when we get there.'

We'd reached Weezer's playground by then and she ran off to find her friends. I went on to the Juniors' playground, thinking to myself: maybe we'll get some chocolate, and anyway, the insides of people's houses are always exciting.

On the day of the dancing display, Weezer wanted to be the first little swan in the changing room, so we had to drive down to the school Miss Matting was using earlier than any of the others. I had to wait about with Weezer while Mum went home again, and came back at a more sensible time with Mrs Posnansky.

Weezer arranged her things (which she kept in a special pink suitcase) on a sort of shelf in front of a big mirror.

'This is a proper drama studio,' she said. 'And this is almost like a real dressing room in a theatre. Last year, at the other school, we had to dress in the girls' toilets.'

'Would you like me to do your hair?' I asked.

'Oh, yes,' said Weezer. 'No one scrapes it back as well as you.'

I combed her hair as smooth and flat as I could, and put an elastic ponytail holder round it.

'Are you doing a bun?' she asked.

'You'll look like Mrs Posnansky,' I said.

'I don't care,' said Weezer. 'I think she's nice.'

She *was* nice. Her powder smelled of icing sugar, and she walked very slowly with a cane. All the furniture in her house was made of dark wood, and Weezer and I had sat on a saggy maroon sofa in her front room, while she went to find the chocolates. She'd been so pleased to be invited to Weezer's display that she'd had to sit down for a few minutes. Weezer interrupted my thoughts.

'And wasn't it lucky I invited her? Her own mother was a dancer once . . . in that ballet in Russia. Isn't that amazing? I can't remember what she called it. Something beginning with B.'

'Bolshoi,' I said. 'Haven't you ever heard of the Bolshoi Ballet? They're ever so famous. I'm surprised Miss Matting hasn't told you about them.'

'Of course she's told us,' Weezer said, brushing

her cheeks furiously with Mum's best blusher.
'I'd just forgotten, that's all.'

I was on the point of saying I didn't believe her
when I thought of how cross she'd be to be
discovered telling a fib. So I shut up for the sake
of the dancing display. I wanted it to go well
now, if only for Mrs Posnansky's sake.

'This invitation,' she'd said, 'it is better than a
box for the Royal Gala. Thank you, Louisa and
Annie.'

The other little swans had arrived by now, and
so had peasants, witches, clowns, cats and other
assorted creatures taking part in the display.

Soon, the dressing room was full of tutus and
lipsticks and chattering high voices, and everyone
was spraying their hair flat and tying up the long
pink satin ribbons on their ballet shoes.

'Zip me up, Annie,' Weezer said.

'You look lovely,' I said, because she did. 'Just
like a fluffy white cygnet.'

'Little swan.'

'Have it your own way.'

Then, there was a knock at the dressing-room
door.

'May we come in?' Mum said. 'Mrs Posnansky
would like to –'

Miss Matting bounded through the crowds of
children to try and stop them getting in. I could

hear my mother whispering, and see Mrs Posnansky nodding, and Miss Matting gasping and covering her mouth with her hand. Mrs Posnansky was in her best clothes, but why had she brought a Tesco carrier bag?

'Children!' Miss Matting called out, and clapped her hands for silence. 'Children, I'd like you all to meet Louisa's special guest. Her name is Nina Posnansky, and she was born in Russia, where the greatest ballerinas came from. Her mother was – oh, this is so exciting – in the *corps de ballet* in Pavlova's time, and danced in *Swan Lake* as one of the little swans! Oh, this is wonderful!'

All the children nodded and smiled and then started clapping Mrs Posnansky. She was beaming and at the same time fishing around in the carrier bag.

'Thank you, children,' she said. 'I have never had applause like this before. Your teacher is right. Natasha Arlozorovska was my mother. This,' (she held up a small white satin headband covered with soft feathers) 'is the headdress she wore in the "Dance of the Little Swans". It was in a big trunk in my attic, but I looked and looked and found it at last. I would be honoured if Louisa would wear it.'

Weezer blushed bright scarlet and ran over to Mrs Posnansky, who fixed the headband round her head.

'Perfect!' said Miss Matting. 'You are the

perfect little swan, Louisa. Now, we're starting in a minute, so say goodbye and thank you to Mrs Posnansky and Mrs Foster. They're going to find their seats now.'

I went with them, and we sat and waited in the dark for the display to begin.

I was surprised to find myself enjoying all the dances, but when Louisa came on with the other little swans in their feathery white dresses, I was amazed. I forgot that she was my stubborn, moody, bossy younger sister because she floated through the music as though her body weighed nothing, and she bent and turned as though her

bones had vanished, and the white headband made her carry her head as gracefully as a real swan. I thought: she deserves to be called Louisa for dancing like that, and I glanced at Mrs Posnansky. Tears were rolling down her cheeks. She must have seen me looking at her, because she turned to face me and whispered:

'I am crying because it is so beautiful!'

The music swelled and filled the hall and the little swans froze into their last positions.

Later I said: 'I shall call you Louisa forever. You were easily the best cygnet of the lot. I expect it was because of the lucky Russian headband.'

'Little swan,' said Weezer happily.

My sister has to have her own way.

I Don't Want to Dance!

Bel Mooney

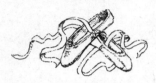

Kitty's cousin Melissa had started ballet classes.

'Why don't you go as well, dear?' suggested Kitty's mum.

'I don't want to dance!' growled Kitty, picking up her biro to draw a skull and crossbones on her hand. Mum sighed, looking at Kitty's tousled hair, dirty nails, and the dungarees all covered in soil – from where Kitty had been playing Crawling Space Creatures with William from next door.

'I think it would be nice for you,' she said, 'because you'd learn . . . you'd learn . . . Well, dancing makes you strong.'

'No,' said Kitty – and that was that.

But when Kitty's big brother Daniel came home from school and heard about the plan, he laughed. 'Kitty go to ballet!' he screamed. 'That's a joke! She'd dance like a herd of elephants!'

Just then Dad came in, and smiled. 'Well, I think she'd dance like Muhammed Ali.'

'Who's he?' Kitty asked.

'He was a boxer,' grinned Dad.

That did it. If there was one thing Kitty hated it was being teased (although to tell the truth she didn't mind teasing other people!). 'Right! I'll show you!' she yelled.

So on Saturday afternoon Kitty was waiting outside the hall with the other girls (and two boys) from the ballet class. Mum had taken her shopping that morning, and Kitty had chosen a black leotard, black tights and black ballet shoes. Now she saw that all the other girls were in pink. She felt like an ink blot.

Mum went off for coffee with Auntie Susan, leaving Kitty with Melissa and her friend, Emily. They both had their hair done up in a bun, and wore little short net skirts over their leotards. They looked Kitty up and down in a very snooty way.

'You could never be a ballet dancer, Kitty, 'cos you're too clumsy,' said Melissa.

'And you're too small,' said Emily.

Kitty glared at them. 'I don't want to dance anyway,' she said. 'I'm only coming to this boring old class to please Mum.'

But she felt horrid inside, and she wished – oh, how she wished! – she was playing in the garden with William. Pirates. Explorers. Cowboys. Crawling Space Creatures. Those were the games they played and Kitty knew they suited her more than ballet class.

She put both hands up to her head and tore out the neat bunches Mum had insisted on. That's better – that's more like *me*, she thought.

Miss Francis, the ballet teacher, was very pretty and graceful, with long black hair in a knot on top of her head. She welcomed Kitty and asked if she had done ballet before.

'No,' said Kitty in a small, sulky voice.

'Never mind,' said Miss Francis. 'You'll soon catch up with the others. Stand in front of me, and watch my feet. Now, class, make rows . . . heels together . . . First position!'

Kitty put her heels together, and tried to put her feet in a straight line, like Miss Francis. But it was very hard. She bent her knees – that made it easier.

There was a giggle from behind.

'Look at Kitty,' whispered Emily. 'She looks like a duck!'

Miss Francis didn't hear. 'Good!' she called. 'Now do you all remember the first position for

your arms? Let's see if we can put it all together . . . '

Kitty looked at the girls each side of her, then at Miss Francis – and put her arms in the air. She stretched up, but was thinking so hard about her arms she forgot what her feet were doing. Then she thought about her feet, and forgot to look up at her arms.

There was an explosion of giggles from behind.

'Kitty looks like a tree in a storm,' whispered Melissa.

'Or like a drowning duck!' said Emily.

'Shh, girls!' called Miss Francis with a frown.

And so it went on. Kitty struggled to copy all the positions, but she was always a little bit behind. Once, when Miss Francis went over to speak to the lady playing the piano, she turned round quickly and stuck her tongue out at Melissa and Emily.

Of course, that only made them giggle more. And some of the other children joined in. It wasn't that they wanted to be mean to Kitty – not really. It was just that she looked so funny, with her terrible frown, and her hair sticking out all over the place. And they thought she felt she was better than all of them. But of course the truth was that the horrible feeling inside Kitty was growing so fast she was afraid it would burst out of her eyes.

Everybody seemed so clever and skilful – except her.

'I *am* an ink blot,' she thought miserably.

It so happened that Miss Francis was much more than pretty and graceful; she was a very good teacher. She saw Kitty's face and heard the giggles, and knew exactly what was going on. So she clapped her hands and told all the children to sit in a circle.

'Now, we're going to do some free dancing,' she said, 'so I want some ideas from you all. What could we all be . . .?'

Lots of hands shot up, because the class enjoyed this. 'Let's do a flower dance,' called Melissa.

'Birds,' suggested Emily.

'Let's pretend we're trees . . . and the hurricane comes,' called out one of the boys.

'I want to be a flower,' Melissa insisted.

Miss Francis looked at Kitty. 'What about you? You haven't said anything,' she said with a smile.

Kitty shook her head.

'Come on, Kitty, I know you must have an idea. Tell me what we can be when we dance. Just say whatever comes into your head.'

'Crawling Space Creatures,' said Kitty.

The children began to laugh. But Miss Francis held up her hand. 'What a good idea! Tell us a little bit about them first, so we can imagine them . . .'

'Well, me and William play it in the garden, and we live on this planet which is all covered with jungle, and we're really horrible-looking things, with no legs, just tentacles like octopuses. And so we move about by crawling, but since we like the food that grows at the top of the bushes we sometimes have to rear up, and that's very hard, see. And we have to be careful, 'cos there's these birds that eat us if they see us, so we have to keep down. Sometimes William is the birds, and tries to get me . . .'

'All right, children – you're all Crawling Space Creatures. We'll see if we can get some spooky, space-like music on the piano . . .'

The lady playing the piano smiled and nodded.

So they began. Most of the children loved the

idea, but Melissa and Emily and two other girls looked very cross and bored.

'Down on the floor, girls!' called Miss Francis.

Kitty had a wonderful time. She listened to the music, and imagined the strange planet, and twisted her body into all sorts of fantastic shapes. After a few minutes Miss Francis told the others to stop. 'All watch Kitty!' she said.

So the children made a circle, and Kitty did her own dance. She lay on the floor and twisted and turned, waving her arms in time to the music. Sometimes she would crouch, then rear up, as if reaching for strange fruit, only to duck down in terror, waving her 'tentacles', as the savage birds wheeled overhead . . .

At last the music stopped, and all the children clapped. Kitty looked up shyly. She had forgotten where she was. She had lost herself in her dance.

When the lesson was over, Miss Francis beckoned Kitty to come over to the piano. None of the children noticed; they were all crowding round the door to meet their mothers.

'Now, Kitty,' said Miss Francis quietly, 'what do you think you've learned about ballet today?'

'It's hard,' said Kitty.

'Well, yes, it is hard. But what else? What about your space dance?'

'That was fun!'

'Because it was *you*?'

Kitty nodded.

'Well, we'll do lots of make-up dances too, and

you'll find you can be lots of things – if you let yourself. That's what modern ballet is all about, you know. Now take this book, and look at the pictures, and you can practise all the positions for next week . . . You are coming next week?'

Kitty nodded happily, and went off to find Mum. Outside in the hall Melissa and Emily glared at her.

'Look at my tights – they're all dirty,' moaned Melissa.

'All that crawling about on the floor – so babyish!' said Emily, in the snootiest voice.

'If you knew anything, you'd know that's what modern ballet is all about,' said Kitty, in her most wise and grown-up voice. 'I shall have to teach you some more about it next week. Now, if you'll just let me past, I'm going to go home and practise.'

The First Night Surprise

Susan Hampshire

It was in the Christmas holidays that Lucy Jane's dream of being a real ballet dancer came true. Although she was only eight she had been chosen to be an understudy in the part of one of the children in *The Nutcracker* ballet at Covent Garden.

Lucy Jane was a little upset that she was only an understudy, but she was very excited to have been chosen. Lucy Jane knew that if one of the girls were ill or did not want to go on, then she would dance in their place. Not knowing if she would dance made it all the more exciting.

Each morning Lucy Jane and her friends Alice, Carole and Celia went to a ballet class and a rehearsal for *The Nutcracker*. Then in the afternoons they would rehearse once more. One of the things Lucy Jane enjoyed most was watching all the grown-up dancers. They were all so friendly and kind to the children. Mimi even gave the girls her last six glucose sweets and shared her orange with Lucy Jane. 'Only five more days to go until the performance,' she said happily as she popped the last segment of orange into her mouth, and did a little pirouette.

The day of the dress rehearsal was filled with a magic all of its own, and although Lucy Jane was not allowed to rehearse this time because none of the girls were ill, she felt a lovely feeling inside. The theatre buzzed with all the excitement and activity of a family getting ready for Christmas.

Most of the dancers of the *corps de ballet* were very helpful and showed the children where to enter the stage, where to rub their feet in the rosin tray so that their ballet shoes would not slip when they danced on stage. They also tried to make sure that they did not have stage fright. All the dancers were in their costumes. There was a full orchestra and all the lights and scenery were there in use exactly as they would be on the first night.

Lucy Jane was very excited and, as she wasn't dancing, one of the assistants took her into the auditorium to watch from the stalls. Sometimes Leonard, the choreographer, would scream, 'Sto-o-p!' from the stalls and everything and everyone would grind to a halt while a problem was sorted out and the stage hands practised bringing on the scenery again. Then the dancers repeated a section of their dance to be sure it was in time with the orchestra.

Lucy Jane wished that she too was dancing on the stage but each time she was about to go off into a little daydream of her own, imagining she was the ballerina, Leonard's voice would be heard screaming about something and his assistant quickly rushed over to calm him down so that the dress rehearsal could start again.

The next day was the first performance. Everyone involved was frantically rushing about. There were all sorts of last-minute errands: the children suddenly needed more hairclips and the men ran out of body make-up. Sarah, the wardrobe mistress, did her best to keep calm in all the pandemonium. She quietly asked the dressers to see to everyone's needs.

The girls' dressing room was right at the top of the building. It was large and bare except for ten old wooden chairs and dressing tables, which were just plain table tops all along one wall. There were no flowers or greetings cards or any of the colourful things that made the star Miss Marova's dressing room look so pretty. Hers was near the stage.

No one was ill, and Lucy Jane was feeling rather left out as she knew she was not going to be in the ballet. She watched a little enviously as the five girls she was understudying put a little rouge on their cheeks and tied ribbons in their hair. She had been given a costume to wear 'just in case'. All Lucy Jane really wanted to do was hide away in the dressing room and cry. But she made a great effort to be cheerful and help the girls change. She brushed their hair and told them how pretty they looked.

The orchestra could be heard tuning up and faint echoes of music drifted up the stairs. The children were all dressed and made-up and the

chaperone, Mrs Stone, who was in charge of the children, sat in the only large and comfortable dressing-room armchair, drinking endless cups of tea from her Thermos. She was knitting a candy-pink dress for her granddaughter.

Suddenly the final announcement came over the loudspeaker: 'Beginners, Act 1, please!' and a flurry of nerves and excitement passed through the girls.

As Alice skipped around excitedly, waiting to go down, she said, 'Wear your dress anyway, Lucy Jane, just for the fun of dressing up, and then it will seem as if we're all going on stage.'

Lucy Jane thought this was a lovely idea, so while her friends practised in the corner, she put on her costume. Then they all huddled in a circle complaining of butterflies in their tummies and chanting, 'I'm glad I'm not playing one of the mice in *The Nutcracker*.' The mice costumes were very hot, especially the headdress, and many of the mice children grumbled about tripping over their tails. Her friends were dancing the part of the children.

Mrs Stone told all the girls except Lucy Jane to go and wait at the side of the stage. So poor Lucy Jane sat quietly alone, longing to join them. She could hear the overture playing, the chaperone's knitting needles clicking and her own feet scratching on the bar across her chair. She was just wondering if she dare put some make-up on her cheeks when suddenly there was a loud knock at the door and the stage doorkeeper's voice shouted, 'Lucy Jane – something for you.'

Lucy Jane rushed to the door and took a large white envelope from his hand. She was so excited, she could hardly tear it open. Inside was a card from Tatiana Marova, the ballerina. It read, 'To my clever little pupil. I'm sorry you won't be dancing today. Maybe another day. Lots of love, Tati and Miss Softpaws, the cat.'

Lucy Jane kissed the card, pushed it down the front of her dress and rushed towards the door. Mrs Stone dropped her knitting and called, 'Where are you going?'

'Downstairs to thank Miss Marova for her card.'

Mrs Stone obviously thought that Lucy Jane had no right to be talking to the star so she told her to come back at once and sit down. Lucy Jane reluctantly did so.

'Rats and rabbits,' Lucy Jane whispered as she folded her arms and plonked herself in the nearest chair. She sat swinging her legs and longing to be out of the old dragon's sight. All Lucy Jane wanted was to be at the side of the stage with the other girls. She so wanted to feel part of the performance.

Suddenly, outside the dressing-room door, there was a tremendous commotion. Lucy Jane nervously jumped to her feet. She felt sure a fire had broken out. She rushed over to Mrs Stone and told her to get her handbag. Then the door

swung open and a breathless, dishevelled company manager hurled himself into the room and grabbed Lucy Jane by the arm. 'Quick, Lucy Jane, run,' he panted.

'I think it's a fire, Mrs Stone, come on. Fire!' Lucy Jane shouted, and they both ran towards the stairs. The company manager anxiously ushered Lucy Jane down first, and Mrs Stone tried to follow, clutching her knitting and her handbag. Then the company manager yelled to Lucy Jane, 'You're on, you're on. If you don't hurry, you'll be off!'

Lucy Jane had no idea what he meant but she

tried to keep up with him as he overtook her and galloped down the steps two at a time. He dragged her through the pass door to the stage and into the wings saying, 'Go on, Alice has just sprained her ankle. Quick, you're on!'

Lucy Jane had no time to be frightened or ask about her friend. She could hear her music so she ran on stage. As she danced into the limelight, everyone crowded into the wings to watch her.

'She's doing beautifully,' said Lillie, Miss Marova's dresser, dabbing her eyes with her handkerchief.

The few steps Lucy Jane had to do, she did perfectly. She felt as if she was floating as she danced and turned in her light-blue dress, with her arms stretched beautifully to the side holding the frill on the hem of her three-quarter-length skirt.

She could feel the spotlight shining on her as she danced and with each point of her foot she enjoyed the feeling of dancing on stage more and more. But, towards the end, there was a soft clattering noise as Miss Marova's card fluttered from Lucy Jane's dress to the floor. At first, Lucy Jane could not imagine what it was, but when she realised she just managed to bend down and pick it up in time to the music. She made the whole movement look like a graceful curtsey, and then as she stepped up stage she quickly pushed it back into the bodice of her dress before anyone noticed.

On the other side of the stage Miss Marova stood watching with tears in her eyes. She was so proud to see her little pupil taking over so perfectly. But what thrilled her most was the way Lucy Jane had made the falling card a natural part of the ballet. Not many first-timers would have done that. As the girls came off stage, Miss Marova hugged them all and gave Lucy Jane a special squeeze.

'Bravo, bravo, my little Lucy Jane!' and so saying she kissed her on both cheeks. 'You are now a real little dancer. You see how important it is to be an understudy?' Lucy Jane nodded.

'But wasn't it awful about the card?' said Lucy

Jane, absolutely ashamed. 'I wanted to keep it near me, so I had it tucked in my dress, but I didn't know that I was going to have a chance to dance.'

'You behaved like a professional,' Miss Marova said proudly.

Sarah, the wardrobe mistress, who was in the wings too, also reassured Lucy Jane. 'You did very well, darling, I'm very proud of you,' she whispered. 'Now you can say, "I am in the ballet!"' and she hugged her.

On the way back to the dressing room upstairs they found Mrs Stone, the chaperone, on the landing holding her handbag and saying, 'I can't smell a fire.'

Lucy Jane shouted to her excitedly as she passed, 'Mrs Stone, I've been on, I've been on stage, Mrs Stone. I'm sorry, Mrs Stone, false alarm, no fire,' and she bounced up the stairs, her heart bursting with excitement.

'I'm a dancer,' she said to herself. 'A real dancer. I've been on stage and danced in *The Nutcracker* at Covent Garden.'

And for Lucy Jane there would never be any more special Christmas holiday than the one when she turned from an understudy into a 'little star'.

Poppy Smith – Prima Ballerina

Jean Ure

One morning Miss Hardcastle said to her class,
'Does anyone here learn ballet? Do we have any
little dancers in our midst?'

There was a silence while everyone looked at
everyone else. Not a hand went up. Pippa Smith's
almost did, but at the last moment she wasn't
quite brave enough. Practising ballet in her
bedroom every night (and sometimes every
morning, too) wasn't really the same as learning
from a proper ballet teacher.

Miss Hardcastle obviously hadn't noticed
Pippa's hand wavering and then collapsing. She
said, 'That's a pity! Miss Wilson up at the big
school is looking for four little dancers for the
Christmas pantomime. I was hoping we might be
able to help. Never mind! I'm sure she'll find
someone from somewhere.'

Pippa's heart thudded and banged against her
ribs. Why hadn't she put her hand up? After all,
she *was* learning ballet – sort of. It was just that
she was learning it by herself.

Last year Pippa had been taken to see a ballet
called *Swan Lake* with a famous ballerina called
Bianca White, and ever since then she had

dreamed of becoming a famous ballerina herself, wearing a white frilly dress (known as a tutu) and dancing on her toes in pink satin shoes, only every time she asked her mum if she could have ballet lessons her mum said, 'We'll have to think about it.'

The truth was that Pippa's mum couldn't afford to pay for Pippa to take proper lessons. That was why Pippa had to practise in her bedroom, in front of a large photograph of Bianca White which she had stuck on her bedroom wall. And now she had missed an opportunity to star in the big school's pantomime, all because she was such a *coward*. She was sure Bianca White wouldn't have been a coward.

Next day Miss Wilson came down from the big school to take Miss Hardcastle's class for a special dancing lesson. (The boys were told they could either dance or play football: every single one of them went off to play football. Silly, boys were.)

'What I'm looking for,' said Miss Wilson, 'are four little princesses.'

Pippa immediately drew herself up straight and tall and did her best to look like Princess Diana. It wasn't easy, because Pippa was rather tiny and thin, with raggedy red hair and a snub nose; not a bit like Princess Diana, or indeed any other princess.

'Don't worry if you've never learnt ballet,' said Miss Wilson. 'Don't let that stop you.'

Pippa didn't. Nothing would have stopped

Bianca White and nothing was going to stop Pippa. By the end of the class she had almost forgotten she was raggedy-haired and snub-nosed. She wouldn't have been at all surprised if someone had curtseyed and called her 'Your Royal Highness'.

Miss Wilson was murmuring to Miss Hardcastle. Miss Hardcastle nodded.

'Angela Phillips!' she said. 'Ayesha Khan! Joyce Chan! Hannah Whitbread! Four little princesses, to dance in the pantomime!'

Pippa's freckledy face turned bright scarlet like a blood orange. Whatever was Miss Wilson thinking of? Angela Phillips was the only one who looked in the least like Princess Diana. Hannah was tall, but she wasn't fair, in fact she was black, and Ayesha Khan was just as tiny as Pippa and Joyce Chan was even tinier than either of them. Miss Wilson must be *mad*.

There was only one thing for it: Pippa would have to show her that in spite of having freckles and a snub nose she was a better princess than any of them!

Once a week, the girls of Pippa's class gathered in the PE hall to learn the dance of the four princesses with Miss Wilson.

'I want everyone to learn,' said Miss Wilson, 'just in case any of my four should go down with the flu.'

Pippa at once started praying: please, please let one of Miss Wilson's four go down with the flu . . .

Unfortunately, they all stayed horribly healthy. In the meanwhile, Pippa did her best to be noticed.

'Glide, glide!' chanted Miss Wilson, as the music for the dance came from the cassette player. 'Slowly, slowly . . . slow and graceful . . . remember, you are princesses!'

Slowly and gracefully, arms held before her, Pippa glided. She was so busy being a princess that she didn't notice Mandy Harris coming towards her in the opposite direction. It was Mandy's fault: Miss Wilson had said turn left and Mandy had turned right. (She always had trouble

with left and right.) *Crash!* went Pippa, gliding
straight into her.

'*Ow!*' screeched Mandy. 'Watch where you're
going!'

Pippa was cross: Mandy had gone and spoilt
her flow.

'Watch yourself, you idiot!'

'Now, now!' said Miss Wilson. She looked at

Pippa, sternly. 'We'll have less of that.'

The next week they learnt the steps for 'Princesses' Playtime'. Each of the princesses had to toss an imaginary ball into the air and catch it as she danced. Pippa tossed and caught, and caught and tossed, and danced just as hard as she could. Her imaginary ball flew far higher than anyone else's, her feet moved far faster. When she leapt she was more vigorous, when she turned she was almost dizzying. Mandy Harris had just better keep out of her way!

'That girl there,' said Miss Wilson, pointing at Pippa. 'Come here, will you, please!'

Proudly, Pippa wiggled her way out to the front. This was the moment she had been waiting for . . . the moment when Miss Wilson said that Pippa Smith must take the place of one of the other princesses!

'What is your name?' said Miss Wilson.

Pippa grinned, broadly. 'Pippa Smith,' said Pippa.

'Pippy Smith?' said Miss Wilson. 'I can see I shall have to keep an eye on you.'

After that, Miss Wilson made Pippa stay at the front where she could see her. And every week, she called her by a different name.

'Pansy Smith, stay in line! Polly Smith, stop showing off!'

She was Pansy and Polly and Petal and Patsy, but she was never asked to be a princess.

On the day of the pantomime, which was a

Saturday, Pippa came in to school early. The show didn't start until two o'clock, but Pippa was there by half-past one. Just in case. (In case one of the princesses should suddenly go down with the flu.)

As she walked along the empty corridors of the big school she heard a strange banging sound coming from behind a door marked 'Girls' Cloakroom'. Pippa crept up and listened. She opened the door and peered round.

'Hello?' said Pippa. 'Is anyone there?'

'Help!' squealed a voice. 'I can't get out!'

Someone was locked in a lavatory! It was Ayesha Khan!

Hooray! This was it – Pippa's big chance! She knew what Bianca White would do. Bianca White wouldn't hesitate.

Pippa turned. She was just about to close the door and tiptoe away – 'Thank goodness Pippa is here!' Miss Wilson would say, as she handed Pippa her princess costume – when from behind her locked door Ayesha started to sob.

Pippa hesitated. Ayesha sobbed pitifully.

'Oh, *bother*!' said Pippa, as she raced off to get help.

Miss Wilson didn't even say thank you; she was too busy rushing Ayesha to the sickroom. Poor Ayesha! She couldn't possibly dance in that state.

'We'll just have to go on with only three,' said Miss Wilson, looking straight through Pippa as she spoke.

Miss Wilson went off with Ayesha. The curtain was due to go up in ten minutes. What would Bianca White do? Pippa knew what Bianca White would do.

Boldly, Pippa marched into the dressing room.

'I've got to dance in place of Ayesha,' she said.

And she did! By the time Miss Wilson arrived back it was too late to stop her: Pippa was already on stage.

Next week in the local paper there was a photograph of the princesses doing their playtime dance. Underneath the photograph it said, 'Four little prima ballerinas'. And then it gave their names: 'Angela Phillips, Hannah Whitbread, Joyce Chan and Poppy Smith'.

Pippa didn't mind that she had become Poppy. Nobody ever went on the stage using their real name. She thought that when she became famous that was what she would call herself: Poppy Smith.

She took the scissors and she took the newspaper and she carefully snipped off all the bits she didn't want (which were all the bits that weren't about Poppy Smith) and then she stuck her photograph on the bedroom wall next to Bianca White, and she stuck her new name underneath it.

Bianca White and Poppy Smith . . . prima ballerinas!

Other books by contributors to
Prima Ballerina

The Lucy Jane ballet stories

by Susan Hampshire
Illustrated by Vanessa Julian-Ottie
Available in Methuen Children's Books and Mammoth

Lucy Jane at the Ballet

Lucy Jane is going to live at the theatre. But she doesn't want to go. She wants to stay with her father and her cat Tilly whilst her mother is in hospital having a baby.

But once she gets inside the Theatre Royal she enters a fairy tale world. There she meets Tatania Marova, the prima ballerina. She takes Lucy Jane under her wing and turns her into a dancer - with thrilling and unexpected results.

Lucy Jane on Television

Lucy Jane is a little wary of spending a holiday alone with her grandmother in Scotland. But when she sees in the local paper that a TV company is looking for girls to star in a costume drama she is determined to get the part – though it's not quite as simple as she first thinks...

A thoroughly enjoyable second adventure for Lucy Jane, who made her debut in the highly successful *Lucy Jane at the Ballet*.

Lucy Jane and the Dancing Competition

Lucy Jane desperately wants to go in for the Golden Star Dancing Festival at the Royal Festival Hall. But first she must pass her ballet exam – and she's just sprained her ankle!

Then there are the pleasures and hard work of the Summer Dance Camp – but who is the spiteful troublemaker trying to sabotage Lucy Jane and her friends' chances?

And when the festival draws near, there's yet another last-minute complication: *will* Lucy Jane be able to enter?

A warm, exciting story about the lovable heroine of *Lucy Jane at the Ballet* and *Lucy Jane on Television*.

The Kitty books

by Bel Mooney
Illustrated by Margaret Chamberlain
Available in Methuen Children's Books and Mammoth

I Don't Want To

Kitty's favourite word is NO! She doesn't want to clean her teeth or wash or eat her vegetables or – worst of all – play with boring cousin Melissa. But saying no gives Kitty more problems than even *she* bargained for – and somehow she always ends up wanting to say yes!

'Kitty is a delightfully whining, nagging and normal heroine – funny and affectionate tales that ring with authentic details of family life.'

Sally Feldman, *Independent*

I Can't Find It

Kitty was always losing things. She wasn't careless, but things she put away very, very carefully just - sort of - moved, all by themselves...Then one day, Kitty finds something no one else can find.

This is the hilarious and touching sequel to *I Don't Want To!*

It's Not Fair!

'It's not fair!' is Kitty's plaintive cry. Why is she the shortest in her class? Why can't anyone in her family take a joke? Why can't she go to bed as late as the boy next door? Why don't holidays last forever?

When one day Kitty's mother echoes Kitty's cry of 'It's just not fair' Kitty thinks up a brilliant idea...

But You Promised

Kitty, Bel Mooney's naughty, messy, lovable heroine, returns in a new set of adventures. This time her cry is 'But you promised!'. She discovers that sometimes grown-ups make promises they can't keep. But then so do children!

'well-observed, amusing stories, just right for reading aloud'

Books for Keeps

Why Not?

Kitty always used to say she didn't want to do this or that. Then there was a change – she wanted to DO things, but the grown-ups wouldn't let her. Instead of saying 'I don't want to!' she found herself asking 'Why not?'. But the reply she always got was 'Because I say so'. But Kitty finds her own way round every obstacle – especially when she goes on holiday and wants to go trick-or-treating...